C000265036

INSIGHTS
Prayer

INSIGHTS

Prayer

What the Bible Tells Us about Prayer

WILLIAM BARCLAY

SAINT ANDREW PRESS
Edinburgh

First published in 2009 by
SAINT ANDREW PRESS
121 George Street
Edinburgh EH2 4YN

Copyright © The William Barclay Estate, 1975, 1976, 2001, 2002, 2003
Layout copyright © Saint Andrew Press, 2009

ISBN 978 0 7152 0887 8

All rights reserved. No part of this publication may be produced or
transmitted in any form or by any means, electronic or mechanical,
including photocopy, recording, or information storage and retrieval
system, without permission in writing from the publisher. This book
is sold subject to the condition that it shall not, by trade or otherwise,
be lent, re-sold, hired out or otherwise circulated without the
publisher's prior consent.

The right of William Barclay to be identified as author of this work has
been asserted in accordance with the Copyright, Designs and Patents
Act 1988.

British Library Cataloguing in Publication Data
A catalogue record for this book is available from the British Library

It is the Publisher's policy to only use papers that are natural and
recyclable and that have been manufactured from timber grown in
renewable, properly managed forests. All of the manufacturing
processes of the papers are expected to conform to the environmental
regulations of the country of origin.

Typeset by Waverley Typesetters, Fakenham
Printed and bound by Bell & Bain Ltd, Glasgow

Contents

Foreword

When William Barclay was Professor of Divinity and Biblical Criticism at Glasgow University, the connection between his academic vocation and his personal faith was ever evident.

Before beginning a lecture, he would say, 'Let us pray', in order that he and his students bore witness to how shared reverence before God's Word was a pre-requisite for understanding it. On the last working day of the week, he would inevitably close the short but essential devotions with the words, 'And now a Friday prayer' – for the encouragement of any in his class who might be preaching on the forthcoming Sunday.

But others who were not theology students would be aware of his commitment to prayer through a swathe of publications produced for organisations such as the Boys' Brigade, in order that the most hesitant of worship leaders might have words which spoke to and for those gathered for God.

This book is not a collection of Barclay's prayers, but rather a sequence of biblical reflections musing on passages in the Gospels where Jesus teaches on or is engaged in prayer, and where the letter writers of the early Church encourage the recipients of their wisdom to attend to both public and private devotional life.

Here we see evident the magnificent repository of learning and wisdom which was Willie Barclay's mind. With equal facility he draws on New Testament scholarship, Greek wisdom traditions, rabbinical thinking, English Literature and the experience of non-European churches. This is what we should expect from one who was a *university* professor – not a narrow or obtuse perspective paying obeisance to the preferred theological flavour of the month, but a rounded, multi-faceted *universal* exploration of scriptural teaching rooted as much in the life of the world as in text books.

Here also we see one of the compelling features of Barclay's mastering of communication. For him, everything to do with faith was important. There was no first and second league of engagement with Scripture or with God. It is as if he is so constantly excited by the subject matter that he hopes to infect the reader with his own sense of wonder at the riches which the Word of God has to offer.

Here we do not find a testament to the author's piety as much as insights into what Paul and especially Jesus believed about praying. As such, we can recognise Willie Barclay fondly espousing the maxim of John the Baptist, namely that 'He must increase, but I must decrease' (St John 3:30).

JOHN L. BELL
June 2009

Publisher's Introduction

In *Insights: Easter*, we read about how Jesus went to the Garden of Gethsemane to pray. He knew he was in danger and he could have escaped. Instead, he went to pray.

What is prayer? Why was it so important, that at this critical moment in his life Jesus opted to pray? And what is the significance of prayer for us?

Insights: Prayer opens with two short verses from Colossians, from which William Barclay distils 'the essence of prayer'. Prayer, according to Barclay, is a search for knowledge; this knowledge must then be applied to our human situation to give us spiritual wisdom; and this wisdom must lead us to do the right thing. Prayer is not, therefore, a wistful escape from reality. It goes hand in hand with action. The essence of prayer, then, is 'knowledge plus power'.

In Gethsemane, Jesus faced his fear. He confided to his friends in words that pointed to his destiny: 'My soul is much distressed with a distress like death.' He poured out the agony of his feelings in prayer, while the disciples fell asleep. This was his final battle, 'the soul's battle in the garden'. The authorities arrived, heavily armed and ready for action. Peter reached for his sword. There was panic and noise and jostling and violence. But Jesus' personal battle had already been won.

Now he was calm. He knew the horror of what lay ahead, but he also knew where his power lay.

Barclay relates this episode to our own lives. The disciples slept, and Jesus had to fight the battle of his soul on his own: 'That is true for us all,' writes Barclay. 'There are certain things we must face and certain decisions we must make in the awful loneliness of our own souls.' And yet, in prayer we are not alone. Jesus put his trust in God: 'a trust which we must also have'.

This story is found in the gospels of Matthew, Mark and Luke. We present all three versions here to show the remarkable wealth of detail that Barclay extracts from a very familiar story.

In his commentary on Matthew, Barclay shows us the agony, loneliness, trust and courage of Jesus: 'No one can read this story without seeing the intense reality of that struggle.'

In Mark, Barclay shows the emotional intensity of Jesus: he did not want to die; he did not fully understand why he had to continue his mission; he submitted to the will of God: 'He only knew beyond a doubt that this was the will of God and that he must go on.'

And, in Luke, Barclay focuses on the phrase 'Your will be done', and the many ways in which it can be interpreted.

So, we are shown in different ways how Jesus took his fears and doubts to God in prayer and moved forward in trust and in the knowledge that he was doing the right thing.

Each of these passages was written at a particular time and place for a particular purpose and readership. To understand the background to each of them, you can read William Barclay's *Daily Study Bible* series. Barclay covered the entire

New Testament, verse by verse, in seventeen fascinating volumes. It was Barclay's great intention to help people to better understand the Bible. We hope you will enjoy them and the insights they bring. They are all available from Saint Andrew Press.

The essence of prayer's request

Colossians 1:9–11

> *That, in fact, is why, from the day we heard about it, we do not cease to pray for you, asking that you may be filled with an ever-growing knowledge of his will, in all spiritual wisdom and understanding, so that you may conduct yourselves worthily of the Lord, and in such a way as to be altogether pleasing to him, bearing fruit in every good work, and increasing in the fuller knowledge of God. May you continue to be strengthened with all strength according to his glorious power, so that you may possess all fortitude and patience with joy.*

IT is a very precious thing to hear the prayers of a saint for friends; and that is what we hear in this passage. It may well be said that this passage teaches us more about the essence of prayer's request than almost any other in the New Testament. From it we learn, as C. F. D. Moule has said, that prayer makes two great requests. It asks for understanding and insight into God's will and then for the power to perform that will.

(1) Prayer begins by asking that we may be filled with an ever-growing knowledge of the will of God. Its great purpose is to know the will of God. We are trying not so much to

1

make God listen to us as to make ourselves listen to him; we are trying not to persuade God to do what we want but to find out what he wants us to do. It so often happens that in prayer we are really saying: 'Your will be changed' when we ought to be saying: 'Your will be done.' The first objective of prayer is not so much to speak to God as to listen to him.

(2) This knowledge of God must be translated into our human situation. We pray for spiritual wisdom and under-standing. *Spiritual wisdom* is *Sophia*, which we could describe as *knowledge of first principles*. *Understanding* is *sunesis*, which is what the Greeks sometimes described as *critical knowledge,* meaning *the ability to apply first principles to any given situation which may arise in life.* So, when Paul prays that his friends may have *wisdom* and *understanding*, he is praying that they may understand the great truths of Christianity and may be able to apply them to the tasks and decisions which meet them in everyday living. It is possible to be an expert in theology and a failure in living, to be able to write and talk about the eternal truths and yet helpless in applying them to the things which meet us every day. Christians must know what Christianity means, not in a vacuum but in the business of living.

(3) This knowledge of God's will, and this wisdom and understanding, must result in right conduct. Paul prays that his friends may conduct themselves in such a way as to please God. There is nothing in this world as practical as prayer. It is not escape from reality. Prayer and action go hand in hand. We pray not in order to escape life but in order to be better able to meet it.

(4) To do this, we need power. Therefore, Paul prays that his friends may be strengthened with the power of God. The

great problem in life is not to know what to do but to do it. For the most part, we are well aware in any given situation of what we ought to do; our problem is to put that knowledge into action. What we need is power – and that we receive in prayer. If God merely told us what his will was, that might well be a frustrating situation; but he not only tells us his will, he also enables us to perform it. As the poet John Drinkwater wrote,

> *Knowledge we ask not, knowledge thou hast lent,*
> *But Lord – the will, there lies our deepest need.*
> *Grant us to build above the high intent –*
> *The deed – the deed.*

Through prayer, we reach the greatest gift in all the world – knowledge plus power.

The three great gifts

Colossians 1:9–11 (*contd*)

WHAT we might call the *asking* part of Paul's prayer ends with a prayer for three great qualities. He prays that his Colossian friends may possess all *fortitude*, *patience* and *joy*.

Fortitude and *patience* are two great Greek words which often keep company. *Fortitude* is *hupomonē* and *patience* is *makrothumia*. There is a distinction between these two words. It would not be true to say that Greek always rigidly observes this distinction; but it is there when the words occur together.

Hupomonē is translated as *patience* in the Authorized Version. But it does not mean patience in the sense of simply bowing our heads and letting the tide of events flow over us. It means not only the ability to bear things but the ability, in bearing them, to turn them into glory. It is a conquering patience. *Hupomonē* is the ability to deal triumphantly with anything that life can do to us.

Makrothumia is usually translated as *long-suffering* in the Authorized Version. Its basic meaning is *patience with people*. It is the quality of mind and heart which enables us to cope with people in such a way that their unpleasantness and malice and cruelty will never drive us to bitterness, that their unwillingness to learn will never drive us to despair, that their folly will never drive us to irritation, and that their unloveliness will never alter our love. *Makrothumia* is the spirit which never loses patience with, belief in and hope for others.

So Paul prays for *hupomonē,* the *fortitude* which no situation can defeat, and *makrothumia*, the *patience* which no person can defeat. He prays that Christians may be such that no circumstances will defeat their strength and no human being will defeat their love. Their fortitude in events and patience with people must be indestructible.

Added to all this, there is *joy*. The Christian way is not a grim struggle with events and with people; it is a radiant and sunny-hearted attitude to life. The Christian joy is joy in any circumstances. As C. F. D. Moule puts it, 'If joy is not rooted in the soil of suffering, it is shallow.' It is easy to be joyful when things go well; but Christian radiance is something which all the shadows of life can never quench.

So the Christian prayer is: 'Make me, O Lord, victorious over every circumstance; make me patient with every person; and give me the joy which no circumstance and no one will ever take from me.'

The charter of prayer

Matthew 7:7–11

> 'Keep on asking, and it will be given you;
> Keep on seeking, and you will find;
> Keep on knocking, and it will be opened to you.
> For everyone that asks receives;
> And he who seeks finds;
> And to him who knocks it will be opened.
> What man is there, who, if his son will ask him for bread, will give him a stone? Or, if he will ask for a fish, will he give him a serpent? If, then, you, who are grudging, know how to give good gifts to your children, how much more will your Father in heaven give good things to them that ask him?'

EVERYONE who prays is bound to want to know to what kind of God they are praying. So we want to know in what kind of atmosphere our prayers will be heard. Are we praying to a grudging God out of whom every gift has to be squeezed and coerced? Are we praying to a mocking God whose gifts may well be double-edged? Are we praying to a God whose heart is so kind that he is more ready to give than we are to ask?

Jesus came from a nation which loved prayer. The Jewish Rabbis said the loveliest things about prayer. 'God is as near to his creatures as the ear to the mouth.' 'Human beings can hardly hear two people talking at once, but God, if all the world calls to him at the one time, hears their cry.' 'A man is annoyed by being worried by the requests of his friends, but with God, all the time a man puts his needs and requests before him, God loves him all the more.' Jesus had been brought up to love prayer; and in this passage he gives us the Christian charter of prayer.

Jesus' argument is very simple. One of the Jewish Rabbis asked: 'Is there a man who ever hates his son?' Jesus' argument is that no father ever refused the request of his son; and God the great Father will never refuse the requests of his children.

Jesus' examples are carefully chosen. He takes three examples, for Luke adds a third to the two Matthew gives. If a son asks for bread, will his father give him a stone? If a son asks for a fish, will his father give him a serpent? If a son asks for an egg, will his father give him a scorpion? (Luke 11:12). The point is that in each case the two things cited bear a close resemblance.

The little, round, limestone stones on the seashore were exactly the shape and the colour of little loaves. If a child asks for bread, will a parent mock that child by offering a stone, which looks like bread but which is impossible to eat?

If a child asks for a fish, will a parent give that child a serpent? Almost certainly, the *serpent* is an *eel*. According to the Jewish food laws, an eel could not be eaten, because an eel was an unclean fish. 'Everything in the waters that does not have fins and scales is detestable to you' (Leviticus 11:12). That regulation ruled out the eel as an article of diet. If a child asks for a fish, will a parent indeed give that child a fish, but a fish which it is forbidden to eat, and which is useless to eat? Would a parent mock a child's hunger like that?

If the child asks for an egg, will the parent give that child a scorpion? The scorpion is a dangerous little animal. In action it is rather like a small lobster, with claws with which it clutches its victim. Its sting is in its tail, and it brings its tail up over its back to strike its victim. The sting can be exceedingly painful, and sometimes even fatal. When the scorpion is at rest, its claws and tail are folded in; and there is a pale kind of scorpion, which, when folded up, would look exactly like an egg. If a child asks for an egg, will a parent mock that child by offering that child a stinging scorpion?

God will never refuse our prayers; and God will never mock our prayers. The Greeks had their stories about the gods who answered people's prayers, but the answer was an answer with a barb in it, a double-edged gift. Aurora, the goddess of the dawn, fell in love with Tithonus, a mortal youth, so the Greek story ran. Zeus, the king of the gods, offered her any gift that she might choose for her mortal lover. Aurora very naturally chose that Tithonus might live forever, but she had forgotten to ask that Tithonus might remain forever young;

and so Tithonus grew older and older and older, and could never die, and the gift became a curse.

There is a lesson here: God will always answer our prayers; *but he will answer them in his way*, and his way will be the way of perfect wisdom and of perfect love. Often, if he answered our prayers as we at the moment desired, it would be the worst thing possible for us, for in our ignorance we often ask for gifts which would be our ruin. This saying of Jesus tells us not only that God will answer, but also that God will answer in wisdom and in love.

Although this is the charter of prayer, it lays certain obligations upon us. In Greek, there are two kinds of imperative: there is the *aorist* imperative, which issues one definite command. 'Shut the door behind you' would be an *aorist* imperative. There is the *present* imperative, which issues a command that a person should always do something or should go on doing something. 'Always shut doors behind you' would be a present imperative. The imperatives here are *present* imperatives; therefore Jesus is saying: 'Go on asking; go on seeking; go on knocking.' He is telling us to persist in prayer; he is telling us never to be discouraged in prayer. Clearly, therein lies the test of our sincerity. Do we really want a thing? Is a thing such that we can bring it repeatedly into the presence of God, for the biggest test of any desire is: can I pray about it?

Jesus here lays down the twin facts that God will always answer our prayers *in his way*, in wisdom and in love; and that we must bring to God an undiscouraged life of prayer, which tests the rightness of the things we pray for, and which tests our own sincerity in asking for them.

The laws of prayer

Mark 11:22–6

> Jesus answered, 'Have faith in God. This is the truth I tell you
> – whoever will say to this mountain, "Be lifted up and be cast
> into the sea," and who in his heart does not doubt, but believes
> that what he says is happening, it will be done for him. So
> then I tell you, believe that you have received everything for
> which you pray and ask, and it will be done for you. And
> whenever you stand praying, if you have anything against
> anyone, forgive it, so that your Father who is in heaven may
> forgive you your trespasses.'

We turn now to sayings which Mark attaches to the story of
the blasting of the fig tree [see *New Daily Study Bible: Mark*].
We have noticed more than once how certain sayings of Jesus
stuck in people's minds although the occasion on which he
said them had been forgotten. It is so here. The saying about
the faith which can remove mountains also occurs in Matthew
17:20 and in Luke 17:6, and in each of the gospels it occurs
in a quite different context. The reason is that Jesus said it
more than once and its real context had often been forgotten.
The saying about the necessity of forgiving one another occurs
in Matthew 6:12 and 14 again in a quite different context. We
must approach these sayings as not so much having to do
with particular incidents, but as general rules which Jesus
repeatedly laid down.

This passage gives us three rules for prayer.

(1) It must be the prayer of faith. The phrase about removing mountains was a quite common Jewish phrase.
It was a regular, vivid phrase for *removing difficulties*. It was
specially used of wise teachers. A good teacher who could
remove the difficulties which the minds of his scholars
encountered was called *a mountain-remover*. One who heard a
famous Rabbi teach said that 'he saw Resh Lachish as if he were
plucking up mountains'. So the phrase means that if we have real
faith, prayer is a power which can solve any problem and make
us able to deal with any difficulty. That sounds very simple,
but it involves two things.

First, it involves that we should be willing to take our
problems and our difficulties to God. That in itself is a very
real test. Sometimes our problems are that we wish to obtain
something we should not desire at all, that we wish to find
a way to do something we should not even think of doing,
that we wish to justify ourselves for doing something to
which we should never lay our hands or apply our minds.
One of the greatest tests of any problem is simply to say,
'Can I take it to God and can I ask his help?' Second, it
involves that we should be ready to accept God's guidance
when he gives it. It is the commonest thing in the world for
people to ask for advice when all they really want is approval
for some action that they are already determined to take. It
is useless to go to God and to ask for his guidance unless
we are willing to be obedient enough to accept it. But if we
do take our problems to God and are humble enough and
brave enough to accept his guidance, there does come the
power which can conquer the difficulties of thought and
of action.

(2) It must be the prayer of expectation. It is the universal fact that anything tried in the spirit of confident expectation has a more than double chance of success. The patient who goes to a doctor and has no confidence in the prescribed remedies has far less chance of recovery than the patient who is confident that the doctor can provide a cure. When we pray, it must never be a mere formality. It must never be a ritual without hope.

A scene from Leonard Merrick's book, *Conrad in Quest of His Youth*, provides a good illustration: ' "Do you think prayers are ever answered?" inquired Conrad. "In my life I have sent up many prayers, and always with the attempt to persuade myself that some former prayer had been fulfilled. But I knew. I knew in my heart none ever had been. Things that I wanted have come to me, but – I say it with all reverence – too late ..." Mr Irquetson's fine hand wandered across his brow. "Once," he began conversationally, "I was passing with a friend through Grosvenor Street. It was when in the spring the tenant's fancy lightly turns to coats of paint, and we came to a ladder leaning against a house that was being redecorated. In stepping to the outer side of it my friend lifted his hat to it. You may know the superstition. He was a university man, a man of considerable attainments. I said, 'Is it possible you believe in that nonsense?' He said, 'N-no, I don't exactly believe in it, but I never throw away a chance.' " Suddenly the vicar's inflexion changed, his utterance was solemn, stirring, devout, "I think, sir, that most people pray on my friend's principle – they don't believe in it, but they never throw away a chance." '

There is much truth in that. For many people prayer is either a pious ritual or a forlorn hope. It should be a thing of burning expectation. Maybe our trouble is that what we want from God is *our* answer, and we do not recognize *his* answer when it comes.

(3) It must be the prayer of charity. The prayers of bitter people cannot penetrate the wall of their own bitterness. Why? If we are to speak with God there must be some bond between us and God. There can never be any intimacy between two people who have nothing in common. The principle of God is love, for he *is* love. If the ruling principle of our hearts is bitterness, we have erected a barrier between ourselves and God. In such circumstances, if our prayers are to be answered we must first ask God to cleanse our hearts from the bitter spirit and put into them the spirit of love. Then we can speak to God and God can speak to us.

All is of God

Romans 8:26–7

> *Even so, the Spirit helps us in our weakness; for we do not know what we should pray, if we are to pray as we ought. But the Spirit himself intercedes for us with groanings which baffle speech to utter; but he who searches the hearts knows the mind of the Spirit, because it is by God's will that he intercedes for those whose lives are consecrated to God.*

THESE two verses form one of the most important passages on prayer in the whole New Testament. Paul is saying that, because of our weakness, we do not know what to pray for, but the prayers we ought to offer are offered for us by the Holy Spirit. The New Testament scholar C. H. Dodd defines prayer in this way: 'Prayer is the divine in us appealing to the Divine above us.'

There are two very obvious reasons why we cannot pray as we ought. First, we cannot pray aright because we cannot foresee the future. We cannot see a year or even an hour ahead; and we may well pray, therefore, to be saved from things which are for our good, and we may well pray for things which would be to our ultimate harm. Second, we cannot pray aright because in any given situation we do not know what is best for us. We are often in the position of children who want something which would be bound only to hurt them; and God is often in the position of parents who have to refuse their children's requests or compel them to do something they do not want to do, because the parents know what is good for them far better than the children themselves.

Even the Greeks knew that. Pythagoras forbade his disciples to pray for themselves, because, he said, they could never in their ignorance know what was appropriate and best for them. Xenophon tells us that Socrates taught his disciples simply to pray for good things, and not to attempt to specify them, but to leave God to decide what the good things were. C. H. Dodd puts it in this way. We cannot know our own real need; we cannot with our finite minds grasp God's plan; in the last analysis, all that we can bring to God is an inarticulate sigh which the Spirit will translate to God for us.

As Paul saw it, prayer, like everything else, is of God. He knew that by no possible human effort can we justify ourselves; and he also knew that by no possible effort of the human intelligence can we know what to pray for. In the last analysis, the perfect prayer is simply: 'Father, into your hand I commend my spirit. Not my will, but yours be done.'

The Christian's prayer

Colossians 4:2–4

> *Persevere in prayer. Be vigilant in your prayer, and let thanks-giving always be a part of it. And at the same time pray for us, that God may open for us a door for the word, that we may speak the secret of Christ now revealed to his own people, that secret for which I am in bonds, that I may make it manifest to all, as I ought to speak.*

PAUL would never write a letter without urging the duty and the privilege of prayer on his friends.

He tells them to persevere in prayer. Even for the best of us, there come times when prayer seems to be unproductive and pointless and to penetrate no further than the walls of the room in which we pray. At such a time, the remedy is not to stop but to go on praying; for in those who pray, spiritual dryness cannot last.

He tells them to be vigilant in prayer. Literally, the Greek means to be *wakeful*. The phrase could well mean that Paul is telling them not to go to sleep when they pray. Maybe he was thinking of the time on the Mount of Transfiguration when the disciples fell asleep and only when they were awake again saw the glory (Luke 9:32). Or maybe he was thinking of that time in the Garden of Gethsemane when Jesus prayed and his disciples slept (Matthew 26:40). It is true that, at the end of a hard day, sleep often comes upon us when we try to pray. And very often there is in our prayers a kind of tiredness. At such a time, we should not try to pray for very long: God will understand the single sentence uttered in the manner of a child too tired to stay awake.

Paul asks for their prayers for himself. We must note carefully exactly what it is that Paul asks for. He asks for their prayer not so much for himself as for his work. There were many things for which Paul might have asked them to pray – release from prison, a successful outcome to his coming trial, a little rest and finally peace. But he asks them to pray only that strength and opportunity may be given to him to do the work which God had sent him into the world to do. When we pray for ourselves and for others, we should ask not for release from any task, but rather for strength to complete the task which has been given us to do. Prayer should always be for power and seldom for release; for conquest, not release, must be the keynote of the Christian life.

The universality of the gospel

1 Timothy 2:1–7

So, then, the first thing I urge you to do is to offer your requests, your prayers, your petitions, your thanksgivings for all men. Pray for kings and for all who are in authority, that they may enjoy a life that is tranquil and undisturbed, and that they may act in all godliness and reverence. That is the fine way to live, the way which meets with the approval of God, our Saviour, who wishes all men to be saved, and to come to a full knowledge of the truth. For there is one God, and one mediator, between God and man, the man Jesus Christ, who gave himself a ransom for all. It was thus he bore his witness to God in his own good times, a witness to which I have been appointed a herald and an envoy (I am speaking the truth: I do not lie), a teacher to the Gentiles, a teacher whose message is based on faith and truth.

Before we study this passage in detail, we must note one thing which shines out from it in a way that no one can fail to see. Few passages in the New Testament so stress the universality of the gospel. Prayer is to be made for *all*; God is the Saviour who wants *all* to be saved; Jesus gave his life a ransom for *all*. As Walter Lock writes in his commentary: 'God's will to save is as wide as his will to create.'

This is a note which sounds in the New Testament again and again. Through Christ, God was reconciling the *world* to himself (2 Corinthians 5:18–19). God so loved the *world* that he gave his Son (John 3:16). It was Jesus' confidence that, if he was lifted up on his cross, sooner or later he would draw *all* people to him (John 12:32).

E. F. Brown calls this passage 'the charter of missionary work'. He says that it is the proof that all are *capax Dei*, capable of receiving God. They may be lost, but they can be found; they may be ignorant, but they can be enlightened; they may be sinners, but they can be saved. George Wishart, the reformer and martyr, and forerunner of John Knox, writes in his translation of the First Swiss Confession: 'The end and intent of the Scripture is to declare that God is benevolent and friendly-minded to mankind; and that he hath declared that kindness in and through Jesus Christ, his only Son; the which kindness is received by faith.' That is why prayer must be made for all. God wants all men and women, and so, therefore, must his Church.

(1) The gospel includes *high and low*. Both the emperor in his power and slaves in their helplessness were included in the sweep of the gospel. Both the philosophers in their wisdom and ordinary men and women in their ignorance need the grace and truth that the gospel can bring. Within the gospel, there are no class distinctions. Monarch and commoner, rich and poor, employer and employee are all included in its limitless embrace.

(2) The gospel includes *good and bad*. A strange malady has sometimes afflicted the Church in modern times, causing it to insist that people must be respectable before they are allowed in, and to look askance at sinners who seek entry to its doors. But the New Testament is clear that the Church exists not only to improve and instruct the good but also to welcome and save the sinner. The missionary C. T. Studd used to repeat four lines of doggerel:

> *Some want to live within the sound*
> *Of Church or Chapel bell;*
> *I want to run a rescue shop*
> *Within a yard of hell.*

One of the great saints of modern times, and indeed of all time, was Toyohiko Kagawa. He went to Shinkawa in Japan to find men and women for Christ, and he lived there in the filthiest and most depraved slums in the world. His biographer W. J. Smart describes the situation: 'His neighbours were unregistered prostitutes, thieves who boasted of their power to outwit all the police in the city, and murderers who were not only proud of their murder record but always ready to add to their local prestige by committing another. All the people, whether sick, or feeble-minded or criminal, lived in conditions of abysmal misery, in streets slippery with filth, where rats crawled out of open sewers to die. The air was always filled with stench. An idiot girl who lived next door to Kagawa had vile pictures painted on her back to decoy lustful men to her den. Everywhere human bodies rotted with syphilis.' Kagawa wanted people like that – and so does Jesus Christ, for he wants *all* people, good and bad alike.

(3) The gospel embraces *Christian and non-Christian*. Prayer is to be made for *all* men and women. The emperors and rulers for whom this letter bids us pray were not Christians; they were in fact hostile to the Church, and yet they were to be carried to the throne of grace by the prayers of the Church. For true Christians, there is no such thing as an enemy in all this world. No one is outside our prayers, for no one is outside the love of Christ, and no one is outside the purpose of God, who wants *all* to be saved.

The way of prayer

1 Timothy 2:1–7 (*contd*)

Four different words for prayer are grouped together. It is true that they are not to be sharply distinguished; nevertheless, each has something to tell us about the way of prayer.

(1) The first is *deēsis*, which we have translated as *request*. It is not exclusively a religious word; it can be used of a request made either to another person or to God. But its fundamental idea is a sense of need. No one will make a request unless a sense of need has already wakened a desire. Prayer begins with a sense of need. It begins with the conviction that we cannot deal with life ourselves. That sense of human weakness is the basis of all approach to God. As Joseph Hart's hymn 'Come ye sinners' has it:

> *Let not conscience make you linger,*
> *Nor of fitness fondly dream;*
> *All the fitness he requireth*
> *Is to feel your need of him.*

(2) The second is *proseuchē*, which we have translated as *prayer*. The basic difference between *deēsis* and *proseuchē* is that *deēsis* may be addressed either to others or to God, but *proseuchē* is never used of anything else but approach to God. There are certain needs which only God can satisfy. There is a strength which he alone can give; a forgiveness which he alone can grant; a certainty which he alone can bestow. It

may well be that our weakness remains with us because we so often take our needs to the wrong place.

(3) The third is *enteuxis*, which we have translated as *petition*. Of the three words, this is the most interesting. It is the noun from the verb *entugchanein*. This originally meant simply *to meet* or *to fall in* with a person; it went on to mean *to hold intimate conversation with a person*; then it acquired a special meaning and meant *to enter into a king's presence and to submit a petition to him*. That tells us a great deal about prayer. It tells us that the way to God stands open and that we have the right to bring our petitions to one who is a king. As John Newton wrote in the hymn 'Come my soul, thy suit prepare':

> *Thou art coming to a King;*
> *Large petitions with thee bring;*
> *For his grace and power are such,*
> *None can ever ask too much.*

It is impossible to ask too much from this king.

(4) The fourth is *eucharistia*, which we have translated as *thanksgiving*. Prayer does not mean only asking God for things; it also means thanking God for things. For too many of us, prayer is an exercise in complaint when it should be an exercise in thanksgiving. Epictetus, not a Christian but a Stoic philosopher, used to say: 'What can I, who am a little old lame man, do, except give praise to God?' We have the right to bring our needs to God, but we have also the duty of bringing our thanksgivings to him.

Prayer for those in authority

1 Timothy 2:1–7 (*contd*)

THIS passage distinctly commands prayer for kings and emperors and all who are set in authority. This was a principle of prime importance for communal Christian prayer. Emperors might be persecutors, and those in authority might be determined to stamp out Christianity. But the Christian Church never, even in the times of the most bitter persecution, ceased to pray for them.

It is extraordinary to trace how, all through its early days, those days of bitter persecution, the Church regarded it as an absolute duty to pray for the emperor and his subordinate kings and governors. 'Fear God', said Peter. 'Honour the emperor' (1 Peter 2:17) – and we must remember that that emperor was none other than Nero, that monster of cruelty. The early Christian theologian Tertullian insists that, for the emperor, Christians pray for 'long life, secure dominion, a safe home, a faithful senate, a righteous people, and a world peace' (*Apology*, 30). 'We pray for our rulers,' he wrote, 'for the state of the world, for the peace of all things and for a the postponement of the end' (*Apology*, 39). He writes: 'The Christian is the enemy of no man, least of all of the emperor, for we know that, since he has been appointed by God, it is necessary that we should love him, and reverence him, and honour him, and desire his safety, together with that of the whole Roman Empire. Therefore we sacrifice for the safety of the emperor' (*Ad Scapulam*, 2). Cyprian, Bishop of Carthage in the third century, writing to Demetrianus, speaks of the Christian Church as 'sacrificing and placating God night and day for your peace and safety' (*Ad Demetrianum*, 20). In AD 311, the Emperor Galerius actually asked for the prayers of the Christians, and promised them mercy and tolerant treatment if they prayed for the state. The second-century Christian writer Tatian says: 'Does the emperor order us to pay tribute? We willingly offer it. Does the ruler order us to render service or servitude? We acknowledge our servitude. But a man must be honoured as befits a man, but only God is to be reverenced' (*Apology*, 4). In the same period, Theophilus of Antioch writes: 'The honour that I will give the emperor is all the greater, because I will not worship him, but I will pray for him. I will worship no one but the true and real God, for I know that the emperor was appointed by him ... Those give real honour to the emperor who are well-disposed to him, who obey him, and who pray for him' (*Apology*, 1:11). And the second-century Christian scholar, Justin Martyr, writes: 'We worship God alone, but in all other things we gladly serve you, acknowledging kings and rulers of men, and praying that they may be found to have pure reason with kingly power' (*Apology*, 1:14, 17).

The greatest of all the prayers for the emperor is in Clement of Rome's First Letter to the church at Corinth, which was written in about AD 90 when the savagery of Domitian was still fresh in people's minds: 'Thou, Lord and Master, hast given our rulers and governors the power of sovereignty through thine excellent and unspeakable might, that we, knowing the glory and honour which thou hast given them, may submit ourselves unto them, in nothing resisting thy will. Grant unto them, therefore, O Lord, health, peace, concord, stability, that they may administer the government which thou hast given them without failure. For thou, O heavenly Master, King of the Ages, givest to the sons of men glory and honour and power over all things that are upon the earth. Do thou, Lord, direct their counsel according to that which is good and well-pleasing in thy sight, that, administering the power which thou hast given them in peace and gentleness with godliness, they may obtain thy favour. O thou, who alone art able to do these things, and things far more exceeding good than these for us, we praise thee through the High Priest and Guardian of our souls, Jesus Christ, through whom be the glory and the majesty unto thee both now and for all generations, and for ever and ever. Amen' (1 Clement 61).

The Church always regarded it as a duty and an obligation to pray for those set in authority over the kingdoms of the earth, and brought even its persecutors before the throne of grace.

The gifts of God

1 Timothy 2:1–7 (contd)

THE Church prayed for certain things for those in authority.

(1) It prayed for 'a life that is tranquil and undisturbed'. That was the prayer for freedom from war, from rebellion and from anything which would disturb the peace of the realm. That is the prayer of good citizens for their country.

(2) But the Church prayed for much more than that. It prayed for 'a life that is lived in godliness and reverence'. Here, we are confronted with two great words which are keynotes of the Pastoral Epistles and describe qualities which not only the ruler but every Christian must long to possess.

First, there is *godliness*, *eusebeia*. This is one of the great and almost untranslatable Greek words. It describes reverence towards both God and other people. It describes that attitude of mind which respects others and honours God. Eusebius, the early Church historian, defined it as 'reverence towards the one and only God, and the kind of life that he would wish us to lead'. To the Greeks, the great example of *eusebeia* was Socrates, whom the Greek historian Xenophon describes in the following terms: 'So pious and devoutly religious that he would take no step apart from the will of heaven; so just and upright that he never did even a trifling injury to any living soul; so self-controlled, so temperate, that he never at any time chose the sweeter in place of the bitter; so sensible and wise and prudent that in distinguishing the better from the worse he never erred' (*Memorabilia*, 4:8:11). *Eusebeia* comes very near to that great Latin word *pietas*, which the classical scholar Warde Fowler describes in this way: 'The quality known to the Romans as *pietas* rises, in spite of trial and danger, superior to the enticements of individual passion and selfish ease. Aeneas's *pietas* became a sense of duty to the will of the gods, as well as to his father, his son and his people; and this duty never leaves him.' Clearly, *eusebeia* is a tremendous thing. It never forgets the reverence due to God; it never forgets the rights due to others; it never forgets the respect due to self. It describes the character of those who never fail God, other people or themselves.

Second, there is *reverence*, *semnotēs*. Here again, we are in the realm of the untranslatable. The corresponding adjective *semnos* is constantly applied to the gods. R. C. Trench, who was Archbishop of Dublin, says that the one who is *semnos* 'has on him a grace and a dignity, not lent by earth'. He says that such a person 'without demanding it challenges and inspires reverence'. Aristotle was the great ethical teacher of the Greeks. He had a way of describing every virtue as the mid-point between two extremes. On the one side there was an extreme of excess and on the other an extreme of want, and in between there was the mid-point, the happy medium, in which virtue lay. Aristotle says that *semnotēs* is the mid-point between *areskeia*, *subservience*, and *authadeia*, *arrogance*. It may be said that for the person who is *semnos* all life is one act of worship; all life is lived in the presence of God; such a person moves through the world, as it has been put, as if it were the temple of the living God, never forgetting the holiness of God or the dignity of others.

These two great qualities are regal qualities which everyone must long to possess and for which everyone must pray.

The peace of believing prayer

Philippians 4:6–7

Do not worry about anything; but in everything with prayer and supplication, with thanksgiving, let your requests be

made known to God. And the peace of God, which surpasses
all human thought, will stand sentinel over your hearts and
minds in Christ Jesus.

FOR the Philippians, life was bound to be a source of worry.
Even to be a human being and so to be vulnerable to all the
chances and the changes of this mortal life is in itself a cause
for worry; and in the early Church, to the normal worry of
the human situation there was added the worry of being a
Christian, which meant taking one's life in one's hands. Paul's
solution is prayer. As M. R. Vincent says in his commentary,
'Peace is the fruit of believing prayer.' In this brief passage,
there is a whole philosophy of prayer.

(1) Paul stresses that we can take *everything* to God in
prayer. As it has been beautifully put, 'There is nothing too
great for God's power; and nothing too small for his fatherly
care.' Children may take anything, great or small, to their
parents, sure that whatever happens to them is of interest
there, their small triumphs and disappointments, their
passing cuts and bruises. In exactly the same way, we may
take anything to God, sure of his interest and concern.

(2) We can bring our prayers, our petitions and our
requests to God; we can pray for *ourselves*. We can pray for
forgiveness for the *past*, for the things we need in the *present*,
and for help and guidance for the *future*. We can take our own
past and present and future into the presence of God. We can
pray for *others*. We can commend to God's care those near and
far who are within our memories and our hearts.

(3) Paul lays it down that '*thanksgiving* must be the
universal accompaniment of prayer'. Christians must feel,
as it has been put, that all through life they are, 'as it were,

suspended between past and present blessings'. Every prayer must surely include thanks for the great privilege of prayer itself. Paul insists that we must give thanks *in everything*, in laughter and in tears, in sorrows and in joys alike. That implies two things. It implies *gratitude* and also *perfect submission* to the will of God. It is only when we are fully convinced that God is working all things together for good that we can really feel the perfect gratitude towards him which believing prayer demands.

When we pray, we must always remember three things. We must remember *the love of God*, which only ever desires what is best for us. We must remember *the wisdom of God*, which alone knows what is best for us. We must remember *the power of God*, which alone can bring about that which is best for us. Everyone who prays with a perfect trust in the love, wisdom and power of God will find God's peace.

The result of believing prayer is that the peace of God will stand like a sentry on guard over our hearts. The word that Paul uses (*phrourein*) is the military word for *standing on guard*. That peace of God, says Paul, as the Revised Standard Version has it, *passes all understanding*. That does not mean that the peace of God is such a mystery that the human mind cannot understand it, although this also is true. It means that the peace of God is so precious that the human mind, with all its skill and all its knowledge, can never produce it. It can never be of our contriving; it is only of God's giving. The way to peace is in prayer to entrust ourselves and all whom we hold dear to the loving hands of God.

A praying Church

James 5:16–18

> *Confess your sins to each other, and pray for each other, that you*
> *may be healed. The prayer of a good man, when it is set to work,*
> *is very powerful. Elijah was a man with the same emotions as*
> *ourselves, and he prayed earnestly that it should not rain, and*
> *for three years and six months no rain fell upon the earth. And*
> *he prayed again and the heaven gave rain; and the earth put*
> *forth her fruit.*

THIS passage contains three basic ideas of Jewish religion.

(1) There is the idea that all sickness is due to sin. It was a deeply rooted Jewish belief that where sickness and suffering existed, there must have been sin. 'There is no death without guilt,' said the Rabbis, 'and no suffering without sin.' The Rabbis, therefore, believed that before people could be healed of their sickness their sins must be forgiven by God. Rabbi Alexandrai said: 'No man gets up from his sickness until God has forgiven him all his sins.' That is why Jesus began his healing of the paralytic by saying: 'Son, your sins are forgiven' (Mark 2:5). The Jews always identified suffering with sin. Nowadays we cannot make this automatic identification; but this remains true – that no one can know any health of soul or mind or body without being right with God.

(2) There is the idea that, to be effective, confession of sin has to be made to other people, and especially to the person wronged, as well as to God. In a very real sense, it is easier to confess sins to God than to confess them to another person, and yet in sin there are two barriers to be removed – the

barrier it sets up between us and God, and the barrier it sets up between us and other people. If both these barriers are to be removed, both kinds of confession must be made. This was, in fact, the custom of the Moravian Church, and John Wesley took it over for his earliest Methodist classes. They used to meet two or three times a week 'to confess their faults to one another and to pray for one another that they might be healed'. This is clearly a principle which must be used wisely. It is quite true that there may be cases where confession of sin to each other may do infinitely more harm than good; but, where a barrier has been erected because of some wrong which has been done, people must put themselves right both with God and with one another.

(3) Above all, there is the idea that no limits can be set to the power of prayer. The Jews had a saying that the one who prays surrounds his house with a wall stronger than iron. They said: 'Penitence can do something, but prayer can do everything.' To them, prayer was nothing less than contacting the power of God; it was the channel through which the strength and grace of God were brought to bear on the troubles and problems of life. How much more must this be so for a Christian?

In *Morte d'Arthur*, Tennyson wrote:

> More things are wrought by prayer
> Than this world dreams of. Wherefore, let thy voice
> Rise like a fountain for me night and day.
> For what are men better than sheep or goats
> That nourish a blind life within the brain,
> If, knowing God, they lift not hands of prayer
> Both for themselves and those who call them friend?

> *For so the whole round earth is every way*
> *Bound by gold chains about the feet of God.*

As the Jews saw it, and as indeed it is, to cure the ills of life we need to be right with God and right with one another, and we need to bring to bear upon others through prayer the mercy and the might of God.

Before we leave this passage, there is one interesting technical fact that we must note. It quotes Elijah as an example of the power of prayer. This is an excellent illustration of how Jewish Rabbinic interpretation developed the meaning of Scripture. The full story is in 1 Kings 17–18. The *three years and six months* – a period also quoted in Luke 4:25 – is a deduction from 1 Kings 18:1. Further, the Old Testament narrative does not say that either the coming or the cessation of the drought was due to the prayers of Elijah; he was merely the prophet who announced its coming and its going. But the Rabbis always studied Scripture under the microscope. In 1 Kings 17:1, we read: 'As the Lord the God of Israel lives, *before whom I stand*, there shall be neither dew nor rain these years, except by my word.' Now the Jewish attitude of prayer was *standing before God*, and so in this phrase the Rabbis found what was to them an indication that the drought was the result of the prayers of Elijah. In 1 Kings 18:42, we read that Elijah went up to Carmel, *bowed himself down upon the earth* and put his face between his knees. Once again, the Rabbis saw here the attitude of agonizing prayer, and so found what was to them an indication that it was the prayer of Elijah which brought the drought to an end.

Unwearied in prayer

Luke 18:1–8

> *Jesus spoke a parable to them to show that it is necessary
> always to pray and not to lose heart. 'There was a judge', he
> said, 'in a town who neither feared God nor respected man.
> There was a widow in the same town who kept coming to him
> and saying, "Vindicate me against my adversary." For some
> time he refused. But afterwards he said to himself, "Even
> though I neither fear God nor respect man, because she bothers
> me, I will vindicate this widow, lest by her constant coming she
> exhausts me."' The Lord said, 'Listen to what the unjust judge
> says. And shall God not vindicate his own chosen ones who cry
> to him day and night, even though he seem to wait for long?
> But when the Son of Man comes will he find faith on earth?'*

This parable tells of the kind of thing which could, and often
did, happen. There are two characters in it.

(1) The *judge* was clearly not a Jewish judge. All ordinary
Jewish disputes were taken before the elders, and not into the
public courts at all. If, under Jewish law, a matter was taken
to arbitration, one man could not constitute a court. There
were always three judges, one chosen by the plaintiff, one by
the defendant, and one independently appointed.

This judge was one of the paid magistrates appointed
either by Herod or by the Romans. Such judges were
notorious. Unless plaintiffs had influence and money to bribe
their way to a verdict they had no hope of ever getting a case
settled. These judges were said to pervert justice for a dish of
meat. People even punned on their title. Officially they were

called *Dayyaneh Gezeroth*, which means judges of prohibitions or punishments. Popularly they were called *Dayyaneh Gezeloth*, which means robber judges.

(2) The *widow* was the symbol of all who were poor and defenceless. It was obvious that she, without resource of any kind, had no hope of ever extracting justice from such a judge. But she had one weapon – persistence. It is possible that what the judge in the end feared was actual physical violence. The word translated, lest she *exhausts* me, can mean, lest she *gives me a black eye*. It is possible to close a person's eye in two ways – either by sleep or by assault and battery! In either event, in the end her persistence won the day.

This parable does not *liken* God to an unjust judge; it *contrasts* him to such a person. Jesus was saying, 'If, in the end, an unjust and rapacious judge can be wearied into giving a widow justice, *how much more* will God, who is a loving father, give his children what they need?'

That is true, but it is no reason why we should expect to get whatever we pray for. Often a father has to refuse the request of a child, because he knows that what the child asks would hurt rather than help. God is like that. We do not know what is to happen in the next hour, let alone the next week, or month, or year. Only God sees time whole, and, therefore, only God knows what is good for us *in the long run*. That is why Jesus said we must never be discouraged in prayer. That is why he wondered if human faith would stand the long delays before the Son of Man should come. We will never grow weary in prayer and our faith will never falter if, after we have offered to God *our* prayers and requests, we add the perfect prayer, *Your* will be done.

The sin of pride

Luke 18:9–14

*Jesus spoke this parable to some who were self-confidently
sure that they were righteous and who despised others. 'Two
men went up to the Temple to pray. The one was a Pharisee,
the other a tax-collector. The Pharisee stood and prayed
thus with himself, "O God, I thank thee that I am not as the
rest of men, thieves, unjust, adulterers, or even as this tax-
collector. I fast twice a week. I give a tenth of all that I get."
The tax-collector stood afar off, and would not lift even his
eyes to heaven, and kept beating his breast and said, "O God,
be merciful, to me – the sinner." I tell you, this man went
down to his house accepted with God rather than the other,
because everyone who exalts himself will be humbled, but he
who humbles himself will be exalted.'*

THE devout observed two or three prayer times daily – in the
morning and the evening and sometimes also at noon. Prayer
was held to be specially efficacious if it was offered in the
Temple and so at these hours many went up to the Temple
courts to pray. Jesus told of two men who went.

(1) There was a Pharisee. He did not really go to pray to
God. He prayed *with himself*. True prayer is always offered
to God and to God alone. A certain American cynically
described a preacher's prayer as 'the most eloquent prayer
ever offered to a Boston audience'. The Pharisee was really
giving himself a testimonial before God.

The Jewish law prescribed only one absolutely obligatory fast – that on the Day of Atonement. But those who wished to gain special merit fasted also on Mondays and Thursdays. It is noteworthy that these were the market days when Jerusalem was full of country people. Those who fasted whitened their faces and appeared in dishevelled clothes, and those days gave their piety the biggest possible audience. The Levites were to receive a tithe of all a man's produce (Numbers 18:21; Deuteronomy 14:22). But this Pharisee tithed everything, even things which there was no obligation to tithe.

His whole attitude was not untypical of the worst in Pharisaism. There is a recorded prayer of a certain Rabbi which runs like this: 'I thank Thee, O Lord my God, that thou hast put my part with those who sit in the Academy, and not with those who sit at the street corners. For I rise early, and they rise early; I rise early to the words of the law, and they to vain things. I labour, and they labour; I labour and receive a reward, and they labour and receive no reward. I run, and they run; I run to the life of the world to come, and they to the pit of destruction.' It is on record that Rabbi Simeon ben Jocai once said, 'If there are only two righteous men in the world, I and my son are these two; if there is only one, I am he!'

The Pharisee did not really go to pray; he went to inform God how good he was.

(2) There was a tax-collector. He stood afar off, and would not even lift his eyes to God. The Authorized and Revised Standard Versions do not even do justice to his humility for he actually prayed, 'O God, be merciful to me – *the* sinner,' as if he was not merely *a* sinner, but *the* sinner

par excellence. 'And,' said Jesus, 'it was that heartbroken, self-despising prayer which won him acceptance before God.'

This parable unmistakably tells us certain things about prayer.

(1) No one who is proud can pray. The gate of heaven is so low that none can enter it save upon their knees. Christina Rossetti's words express all that any of us can say:

> *None other Lamb, none other Name,*
> > *None other Hope in heaven or earth or sea,*
> *None other Hiding-place from guilt and shame,*
> > *None beside Thee.*

(2) No one who despises others can pray. In prayer we do not lift ourselves above others. We remember that we are one of a great army of sinning, suffering, sorrowing humanity, all kneeling before the throne of God's mercy.

(3) True prayer comes from setting our lives beside the life of God. No doubt all that the Pharisee said was true. He did fast; he did meticulously give tithes; he was not like other people; still less was he like that tax-collector. But the question is not, 'Am I as good as my neighbour?' The question is, 'Am I as good as God?' Once I made a journey by train to England. As we passed through the Yorkshire moors I saw a little whitewashed cottage and it seemed to me to shine with an almost radiant whiteness. Some days later I made the journey back to Scotland. The snow had fallen and was lying deep all around. We came again to the little white cottage, but this time its whiteness seemed drab and soiled and almost grey in comparison with the pure whiteness of the driven snow.

It all depends what we compare ourselves with. And when we set our lives beside the life of Jesus and beside the holiness of God, all that is left to say is, 'God be merciful to me – the sinner.'

Jesus' prayer for his disciples

John 17:9–19

'It is for them that I pray. It is not for the world that I pray, but for those whom you have given me because they are yours. All that I have is yours, and all that you have is mine. And through them glory has been given to me. I am no longer in the world and they are no longer in the world, and I go to you. Holy Father, keep them in your name, which you gave to me, that they may be one, as we are one. When I was with them I kept them in your name, which you gave to me. I guarded them and none of them went lost, except the one who was destined to be lost – and this happened that the Scriptures might be fulfilled. And now I come to you. I am saying these things while I am still in the world that they may have my joy completed in themselves. I gave them your word, and the world hated them, because they are not of the world. I do not ask that you should take them out of the world, but that you should preserve them from the evil one. They are not of the world, just as I am not of the world. Consecrate them by the truth; your word is truth. As you send me into the world, I send them

into the world. And for their sakes I consecrate myself, that
they too may be consecrated by the truth.'

HERE is a passage closely packed with truths so great that we can
grasp only fragments of them.

First of all, it tells us something about the disciple of
Jesus.

(1) The disciple is given to Jesus by God. What does that
mean? It means that the Spirit of God moves our hearts to
respond to the appeal of Jesus.

(2) Through the disciple, glory has come to Jesus. The
patient who has been cured brings honour to a doctor; the
former pupil who becomes a scholar brings honour to the
teacher; the successful athlete brings honour to the trainer.

The men and women whom Jesus has redeemed bring
honour to him. The bad person made good is the honour
of Jesus.

(3) Disciples are those who are commissioned to a task.
As God sent out Jesus, so Jesus sends out his disciples. Here
is the explanation of a puzzling thing in this passage. Jesus
begins by saying that he does not pray for the world; and yet
he came because God so loved the world. But in John's gospel
the world stands for 'human society organizing itself without
God'. What Jesus does for the world is to send out his disciples
into it, in order to lead it back to God and to make it aware
of God. He prays for his disciples in order that they may be
such as to win the world for him.

Further, this passage tells us that Jesus offered his disciples
two things.

(1) He offered them his *joy*. All he was saying to them
was designed to bring them joy.

(2) He also offered them *warning*. He told them that they were different from the world, and that they could not expect anything else but hatred from it. Their values and standards were different from the world's. But there is a joy in battling against the storm and struggling against the tide; it is by facing the hostility of the world that we enter into the Christian joy.

Still further, in this passage Jesus makes the greatest claim he ever made. He prays to God and says: 'All that I have is yours, and all that you have is mine.' The first part of that sentence is natural and easy to understand, for all things belong to God, and again and again Jesus had said so. But the second part of this sentence is the astonishing claim – 'All that you have is mine.' Martin Luther said: 'This no creature can say with reference to God.' Never did Jesus so vividly lay down his oneness with God. He is one with him to such a degree that he exercises his very power and prerogatives.

Jesus' prayer for his disciples

John 17:9–19 (*contd*)

THE great interest of this passage is that it tells us of the things for which Jesus prayed for his disciples.

(1) The first essential is to note that Jesus did not pray that his disciples should be taken out of this world. He never prayed that they might find escape; he prayed that they might

find victory. The kind of Christianity which buries itself in a monastery or a convent would not have seemed Christianity to Jesus at all. The kind of Christianity which finds its essence in prayer and meditation and in a life withdrawn from the world would have seemed to him a sadly truncated version of the faith he died to bring. He insisted that it was in the rough and tumble of life that a people must live out their Christianity.

Of course there is need of prayer and meditation and quiet times, when we shut the door upon the world to be alone with God, but all these things are not the end that we seek in life, but means to that end; and the end is to demonstrate the Christian life in the ordinary work of the world. Christianity was never meant to withdraw people from life, but to equip them better for it. It does not offer us release from problems, but a way to solve them. It does not offer us an easy peace, but a triumphant warfare. It does not offer us a life in which troubles are escaped and evaded, but a life in which troubles are faced and conquered. However much it may be true that Christians are not of the world, it remains true that it is within the world that their Christianity must be lived out. We must never desire to abandon the world, but always desire to win it.

(2) Jesus prayed for the unity of his disciples. Where there are divisions, where there is exclusiveness, where there is competition between the churches, the cause of Christianity is harmed and the prayer of Jesus frustrated. The gospel cannot truly be preached in any congregation which is not one united band of brothers and sisters. The world cannot be evangelized by competing churches. Jesus prayed that his disciples might be as fully one as he and the

Father are one; and there is no prayer of his which has been so hindered from being answered by individual Christians and by the churches than this.

(3) Jesus prayed that God would protect his disciples from the attacks of the evil one. The Bible is not a speculative book; it does not discuss the origin of evil; but it is quite certain that in this world there is a power of evil which is in opposition to the power of God. It is uplifting to feel that God is the sentinel who stands over our lives to guard us from the assaults of evil. The fact that we fall so often is due to the fact that we try to meet life in our own strength and forget to seek the help and to remember the presence of our protecting God.

(4) Jesus prayed that his disciples might be consecrated by the truth. The word for *to consecrate* is *hagiazein*, which comes from the adjective *hagios*. In the Authorized Version, *hagios* is usually translated as *holy*, but its basic meaning is *different* or *separate*. So, *hagiazein* has two ideas in it.

(a) It means *to set apart for a special task*. When God called Jeremiah, he said to him: 'Before I formed you in the womb I knew you, and before you were born I consecrated you; I appointed you a prophet to the nations' (Jeremiah 1:5). Even before his birth, God had set Jeremiah apart for a special task. When God was instituting the priesthood in Israel, he told Moses to *ordain* the sons of Aaron and to *consecrate* them that they might serve in the office of the priests (Exodus 28:41). Aaron's sons were to be set apart for a special office and a special duty.

(b) But *hagiazein* means not only to set apart for some special office and task, it also means *to equip people with the qualities of mind and heart and character which are necessary for that task*. If they are to serve God, they must have something of God's goodness and God's wisdom in them. Those who would serve the holy God must themselves be holy too. And so God does not only choose people for his special service, and set them apart for it; he also equips them with the qualities needed to carry it out.

We must always remember that God has chosen us and dedicated us for his special service. That special service is that we should love and obey him and should bring others to do the same. And God has not left us to carry out that great task in our own strength, but out of his grace he fits us for our task, if we place our lives in his hands.

The soul's battle in the garden

Matthew 26:36–46

> *Then Jesus went with them to a place called Gethsemane, and he said to his disciples: 'Sit here, while I go away and pray in this place.' So he took Peter and the two sons of Zebedee, and began to be distressed and in sore trouble. Then he said to them: 'My soul is much distressed with a distress like death. Stay here, and watch with me.' He went a little way forward and fell on his face in prayer. 'My Father,' he said, 'if it is possible, let this cup pass from me. But let it be not as I will, but as you will.' He came*

to his disciples, and he found them sleeping, and he said to
Peter: 'Could you not stay awake with me for this – for one
hour? Watch and pray lest you enter into testing. The spirit
is eager, but the flesh is weak.' He went away a second time
and prayed. 'My Father,' he said, 'if it is not possible for this
to pass from me unless I drink it, your will be done.' He came
again and found them sleeping, for their eyes were weighted
down. He left them, and went away again, and prayed the
third time, saying the same words over again. Then he came
to his disciples and said to them: 'Sleep on now and take your
rest. Look you, the hour is near, and the Son of Man is being
delivered into the hands of sinners. Rise; let us go; look you,
he who betrays me is near.'

SURELY this is a passage which we must approach upon our
knees. Here, study should pass into wondering adoration.

In Jerusalem itself, there were no gardens of any size,
for a city set on the top of a hill has no room for open
spaces; every inch is of value for building. So, it came
about that wealthy citizens had their private gardens on
the slopes of the Mount of Olives. The word *Gethsemane*
very probably means an *olive vat*, or an *olive press*; and no
doubt it was a garden of olives to which Jesus had the right
of entry. It is a strange and a lovely thing to think of the
nameless friends who rallied round Jesus in the last days.
There was the man who gave him the donkey on which he
rode into Jerusalem; there was the man who gave him the
upper room where the Last Supper was eaten; and now there
is the man who gave him the right of entry to the garden on
the Mount of Olives. In a desert of hatred, there were still
oases of love.

Into the garden, he took the three who had been with him on the Mount of Transfiguration, and there he prayed; more, he wrestled in prayer. As we look with awed reverence on the battle of Jesus' soul in the garden, we see certain things.

(1) We see the *agony* of Jesus. He was now quite sure that death lay ahead. Its very breath was on him. No one wants to die at thirty-three; and least of all does anyone want to die in the agony of a cross. Here, Jesus had his supreme struggle to submit his will to the will of God. No one can read this story without seeing the intense reality of that struggle. This was no play-acting; it was a struggle in which the outcome swayed in the balance. The salvation of the world was at risk in the Garden of Gethsemane, for even then Jesus might have turned back, and God's purpose would have been frustrated.

At this moment, all that Jesus knew was that he must go on, and ahead there lay a cross. In all reverence, we may say that here we see Jesus learning the lesson that everyone must some day learn – how to accept what he could not understand. All he knew was that the will of God imperiously summoned him on. Things happen to every one of us in this world that we cannot understand; it is then that faith is tried to its utmost limits; and at such a time it is sweetness to the soul that in Gethsemane Jesus went through that too. Writing at the end of the second century, the Church Father Tertullian (*De Baptismo*, 20) tells us of a saying of Jesus, which is not in any of the gospels: 'No one who has not been tempted can enter the kingdom of heaven.' That is, we all have our own private Gethsemane, and each one of us has to learn to say: 'Your will be done.'

(2) We see the *loneliness* of Jesus. He took with him his three chosen disciples; but they were so exhausted that they

could not stay awake. And Jesus had to fight his battle all alone. That also is true for us all. There are certain things we must face and certain decisions we must make in the awful loneliness of our own souls; there are times when other helpers fail and comforts flee; but in that loneliness there is for us the presence of one who, in Gethsemane, experienced it and came through it.

(3) Here we see the *trust* of Jesus. We see that trust even better in Mark's account, where Jesus begins his prayer: '*Abba*, Father' (Mark 14:36). There is a world of loveliness in this word *Abba*, which to western ears is altogether hidden, unless the facts about it are known. The German scholar Joachim Jeremias, in his book *The Parables of Jesus*, writes: 'Jesus' use of the word *Abba* in addressing God is unparalleled in the whole of Jewish literature. The explanation of this fact is to be found in the statement of the fathers Chrysostom, Theodore, and Theodoret that *Abba* (as *jaba* is still used today in Arabic) was the word used by a young child to its father; it was an everyday family word, which no one had ventured to use in addressing God. Jesus did. He spoke to his heavenly Father in as childlike, trustful, and intimate a way as a little child to its father.'

We know how our children speak to us and what they call those among us who are fathers. That is the way in which Jesus spoke to God. Even when he did not fully understand, even when his one conviction was that God was urging him to a cross, he called *Abba*, as a little child might call. Here indeed is trust, a trust which we must also have in that God whom Jesus taught us to know as Father.

(4) We see the *courage* of Jesus. 'Rise,' said Jesus, 'let us be going. He who betrays me is near.' Celsus, the pagan

philosopher who attacked Christianity, used that sentence as an argument that Jesus tried to run away. It is the very opposite. 'Rise,' he said. 'The time for prayer and the time for the garden is past. Now is the time for action. Let us face life at its grimmest and human beings at their worst.' Jesus rose from his knees to go out to the battle of life. That is what prayer is for. In prayer, we kneel before God that we may stand erect before the world. In prayer, we enter heaven that we may face the battles of earth.

Your will be done (1)

Mark 14:32–42

They came to a place the name of which is Gethsemane. Jesus said to his disciples, 'Sit here while I pray.' He took Peter and James and John with him, and began to be in great distress and trouble of mind. He said to them, 'My soul is sore grieved even to death. Stay here and watch.' He went on a little farther and fell on the ground and prayed that, if it was possible, this hour might pass from him. He said, 'Abba, Father, everything is possible to you. Take this cup from me – but not what I wish, but what you wish.' He came and found them sleeping and he said to Peter, 'Simon, are you sleeping? Could you not stay awake for one hour? Watch and pray lest you enter into some testing time. The spirit is willing but the flesh is weak.' And again he went away and prayed in the same words. And again he came and found them sleeping, for their eyes were weighed down with sleep. And they did not know how to answer him. And he came the third time and said to them, 'Sleep on now. Take your rest. It is enough. The hour has come. See! The Son of Man is betrayed into the hands of sinners. Rise! Let us be going! He who betrays me has come!'

THIS is a passage we almost fear to read, for it seems to intrude into the private agony of Jesus.

To have stayed in the upper room would have been dangerous. With the authorities on the watch for him, and with Judas bent on treachery, the upper room might have been raided at any time. But Jesus had another place to which to go. The fact that Judas knew to look for him in Gethsemane shows that Jesus was in the habit of going there. In Jerusalem itself there were no gardens. The city was too crowded, and there was a strange law that the city's sacred soil might not be polluted with manure for the gardens. But some of the rich people possessed private gardens out on the Mount of Olives, where they took their rest. Jesus must have had some wealthy friend who gave him the privilege of using his garden at night.

When Jesus went to Gethsemane there were two things he sorely desired. He wanted *human fellowship* and he wanted *God's fellowship*. 'It is not good that the man should be alone,' God said in the beginning (Genesis 2:18). In time of trouble we want friends with us. We do not necessarily want them to do anything. We do not necessarily even want to talk to them or have them talk to us. We only want them there.

Jesus was like that. It was strange that men who so short a time before had been protesting that they would die for him could not stay awake for him one single hour. But none can blame them, for the excitement and the tension had drained their strength and their resistance.

Certain things are clear about Jesus in this passage.

(1) He did not want to die. He was thirty-three and no one wants to die with life just opening on to the best of the years. He had done so little and there was a world waiting to be saved. He knew what crucifixion was like and he shuddered at the thought of it. He had to compel himself to go on – just as we have so often to do.

(2) He did not fully understand why this had to be. He only knew beyond a doubt that this was the will of God and that he must go on. Jesus, too, had to make the great venture of faith, he had to accept – as we so often have to do – what he could not understand.

(3) He submitted to the will of God. *Abba* is the Aramaic for *my father*. It is that one word which made all the difference. Jesus was not submitting to a God who made a cynical sport of men and women. Thomas Hardy finishes his novel *Tess of the D'Urbervilles*, after telling of her tragic life, with the terrible sentence, 'The President of the Immortals had finished his sport with Tess.' But Jesus was not submitting to a God who was an iron fate such as Edward Fitzgerald portrays in *The Rubaiyat of Omar Khayyam*:

> But helpless pieces of the game he plays,
>> Upon this chequer board of nights and days,
>> Hither and thither moves and checks and slays –
> And one by one back in the closet lays.

God was not like that. Even in this terrible hour, when he was making this terrible demand, God was *father*. When Richard Cameron, the covenanter, was killed, his head and hands were cut off by one Murray and taken to Edinburgh. 'His father being in prison for the same cause, the enemy carried them to him, to add grief unto his former sorrow, and inquired if he knew them. Taking his son's head and hands, which were very fair (being a man of a fair complexion like himself) he kissed them and said, "I know them – I know them. They are my son's – my own dear son's. It is the Lord. Good is the will of the Lord, who cannot wrong me nor mine, but hath made goodness and mercy to follow us all our days."' If we can call God *father* everything becomes bearable. Time and again we will not understand, but always we will be certain that 'The Father's hand will never cause his child a needless tear.' That is what Jesus knew. That is why he could go on – and it can be so with us.

We must note how the passage ends. The traitor and his gang had arrived. What was Jesus' reaction? Not to run away, although even then, in the night, it would have been easy to escape. His reaction was *to face them*. To the end, he would neither turn aside nor turn back.

Your will be done (2)

Luke 22:39–46

> Jesus went out, and, as his custom was, made his way to the
> Mount of Olives. The disciples, too, accompanied him. When
> he came to the place, he said to them, 'Pray that you may not
> enter into temptation.' And he was withdrawn from them,
> about a stone's throw, and he knelt and prayed. 'Father,' he
> said, 'if it is your will, take this cup from me; but not my
> will, but yours be done.' And an angel from heaven appeared
> strengthening him. He was in an agony, and he prayed still
> more intensely, and his sweat was as drops of blood falling
> upon the ground. So he rose from prayer and came to his
> disciples, and found them sleeping from grief. 'Why are you
> sleeping?' he said to them. 'Rise and pray that you may not
> enter into temptation.'

THE space within Jerusalem was so limited that there was no
room for gardens. Many well-to-do people, therefore, had
private gardens out on the Mount of Olives. Some wealthy
friend had given Jesus the privilege of using such a garden,
and it was there that Jesus went to fight his lonely battle.
He knew what crucifixion was like; he had seen it. He was
in an *agony*; the Greek word is used of someone fighting a
battle with sheer fear. There is no scene like this in all history.
This was the very hinge and turning point in Jesus' life. He
could have turned back even yet. He could have refused
the cross. The salvation of the world hung in the balance
as the Son of God literally sweated it out in Gethsemane;
and he won.

A famous pianist said of Chopin's nocturne in C sharp minor, 'I must tell you about it. Chopin told Liszt, and Liszt told me. In this piece all is sorrow and trouble. Oh such sorrow and trouble! – until he begins to speak to God, to pray; then it is all right.' That is the way it was with Jesus. He went into Gethsemane in the dark; he came out in the light – because he had talked with God. He went into Gethsemane in an agony; he came out with the victory won and with peace in his soul – because he had talked with God.

It makes all the difference what tone of voice is used when saying, 'Your will be done.'

(1) It may be said in a tone of helpless submission, as by one who is in the grip of a power against which it is hopeless to fight. The words may be the death-knell of hope.

(2) It may be said as by one who has been battered into submission. The words may be the admission of complete defeat.

(3) It may be said as by one who has been utterly frustrated and who sees that the dream can never come true. The words may be those of a bleak regret or even of a bitter anger which is all the more bitter because nothing can be done about it.

(4) It may be said with the accent of perfect trust. That is how Jesus said it. He was speaking to one who was Father; he was speaking to a God whose everlasting arms were underneath and about him even on the cross. He was submitting, but he was submitting to the love that would never let him go. Life's hardest task is to accept what we cannot understand; but we can do even that if we are sure enough of the love of God. As Robert Browning wrote in 'Paracelsus':

God, thou art love! I build my faith on that …
I know thee, who has kept my path, and made
Light for me in the darkness, tempering sorrow
So that it reached me like a solemn joy:
It were too strange that I should doubt thy love.

Jesus spoke like that; and when we can speak like that, we can look up and say in perfect trust, 'Your will be done.'

Further Reading

The passages in this book are taken from the following volumes of the **New Daily Study Bible Series**. Each of these books will set the passage in its scriptural context.

The Gospel of Matthew Vol. 1
The Gospel of Matthew Vol. 2
The Gospel of Mark
The Gospel of Luke
The Gospel of John Vol. 2
The Letter to the Romans
The Letters to the Philippians, Colossians and
    Thessalonians
The Letters to Timothy, Titus and Philemon
The Letters to James and Peter

William Barclay

A full range of books by William Barclay is available from Saint Andrew Press.

Check our website www.standrewpress.com for details and updates.

Prayer

More Than Words is a collection of 400 prayers for every occasion, addressing contemporary issues with everyday language, using scripture readings and prayer activities to help you to connect your own circumstances with the Word of God.

The Book of Common Order is a volume of liturgy and prayers for churches and individuals.

Worship Anthology is a collection of modern prayers, stories, services and parables written by women for today's Christian.

Christian Prayer for Today is a thoughtful, original approach to prayer by Frank Whaling.

ALSO IN THE *INSIGHTS* SERIES

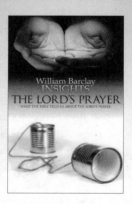

The Lord's Prayer

What the Bible Tells Us about the Lord's Prayer

WILLIAM BARCLAY

Foreword by
RICHARD HARRIES

978-0-7152-0859-5 (paperback)

See our website for details.
www.churchofscotland.org.uk/standrewpress

SAINT ANDREW PRESS

ALSO IN THE *INSIGHTS* SERIES

Christmas

What the Bible Tells Us about the Christmas Story

WILLIAM BARCLAY

Foreword by
NICK BAINES

978-0-7152-0858-8 (paperback)

See our website for details.
www.churchofscotland.org.uk/standrewpress

SAINT ANDREW PRESS

ALSO IN THE *INSIGHTS* SERIES

Easter

What the Bible Tells Us about the Easter Story

WILLIAM BARCLAY

Foreword by
DIANE LOUISE JORDAN

978-0-7152-0860-1 (paperback)

See our website for details.
www.churchofscotland.org.uk/standrewpress

SAINT ANDREW PRESS

ALSO IN THE *INSIGHTS* SERIES

Money

What the Bible Tells Us about Wealth and Possessions

WILLIAM BARCLAY

Foreword by
SALLY MAGNUSSON

978-0-7152-0885-4 (paperback)

See our website for details.
www.churchofscotland.org.uk/standrewpress

SAINT ANDREW PRESS

ALSO BY WILLIAM BARCLAY

If you enjoyed these Insights,
then you will love

The New Daily Study Bible series

*17 classic commentaries
on the New Testament*

WILLIAM BARCLAY

See our website for details.
www.churchofscotland.org.uk/standrewpress

SAINT ANDREW PRESS

ALSO BY WILLIAM BARCLAY

A Beginner's Guide to the New Testament

WILLIAM BARCLAY

978-0-7152-0840-3 (paperback)

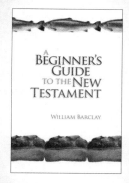

'Anyone can simply open the Bible and read it. But the more we know about the Bible, the more thrilling and fascinating this book becomes. It makes all the difference who said a thing; it makes all the difference when it was said; it makes all the difference where it was said.'

William Barclay

See our website for details.
www.churchofscotland.org.uk/standrewpress

SAINT ANDREW PRESS